to'Be!

Manners
at a
Friend's House

by Amanda Doering Tourville   illustrated by Chris Lensch

PICTURE WINDOW BOOKS
Minneapolis, Minnesota

Special thanks to our advisers for their expertise:

Kay A. Augustine, Ed.S.
National Character Development Consultant and Trainer
West Des Moines, Iowa

Terry Flaherty, Ph.D., Professor of English
Minnesota State University, Mankato

Editor: Shelly Lyons
Designer: Tracy Davies
Page Production: Melissa Kes
Art Director: Nathan Gassman
Editorial Director: Nick Healy
The illustrations in this book were created digitally.

Picture Window Books
151 Good Counsel Drive
P.O. Box 669
Mankato, MN 56002-0669
877-845-8392
www.capstonepub.com

Library of Congress Cataloging-in-Publication Data
Tourville, Amanda Doering, 1980-
Manners at a friend's house / by Amanda Doering Tourville ;
illustrated by Chris Lensch.
p. cm. — (Way to Be!)
Includes index.
ISBN 978-1-4048-5305-8 (library binding)
ISBN 978-1-4048-5306-5 (paperback)
ISBN 978-1-4048-7349-0 (paperback)
1. Etiquette for children and teenagers. 2. Friends—Juvenile literature.
3. Home—Juvenile literature. I. Lensch, Chris. II. Title.
BJ1857.C5T68 2009
395.5—dc22   2008039130

Printed in China.
082011
006251

It's fun to play at a friend's house. If you want to be invited back, you must use good manners. By being polite and respectful to your friend and his or her family, everyone has a good time.

There are lots of ways you can use good manners at a friend's house.

Jack is going to his friend Anna's house. When he arrives, Jack takes off his shoes by the door. He puts them on the rug.

He is using good manners.

Jack has not met Anna's parents before.
He introduces himself.

"Hi, Mr. and Mrs. Yang," Jack says.
"My name is Jack. It's nice to meet you."

Jack is using good manners.

Jack and Anna go outside to play ball.
Anna's little brother wants to play, too.

"Sure, you can play with us," says Jack.

Jack is using good manners.

Anna's dad calls the kids in for dinner. Jack and Anna wash their hands before eating.

They are using good manners.

Jack can't reach all of the food on the table.

"Will you please pass the potatoes?" Jack asks.

"No problem," says Anna.

"Thank you," answers Jack.

Jack is using good manners.

Jack thanks Anna's parents when he's done eating.

"Thank you for dinner, Mr. and Mrs. Yang," Jack says. "The food was very good."

Jack is using good manners.

Jack and Anna help clear the table after dinner. Jack rinses his plate and silverware.

They are using good manners.

Jack and Anna play a video game. They play quietly, because Anna's baby sister is sleeping.

They are using good manners.

It is time for Jack to go home.

"Thank you for inviting me over," Jack tells Anna. "I will ask my parents if you can come to my house next Friday."

He is using good manners.

It is important to use good manners at a friend's house. Using good manners shows that you respect your friends and their families. It also makes everyone feel good.

22

Fun Facts

In the United States, it is polite to pass food to your right before eating.

In the United States, guests often bring a small gift for their host or hostess.

In Morocco, it is polite to say goodbye to each person in the group when leaving a gathering.

In Japan, it is polite to eat every grain of rice in your bowl.

In the United States, it is polite to call before stopping in to visit a friend.

In some South American countries, it is considered rude to rest your hands in your lap at dinner.

To Learn More

More Books to Read

Allen, Kathryn Madeline. *This Little Piggy's Book of Manners.*
    New York: H. Holt, 2003.

Richardson, Adele. *Manners at Home.* Mankato, Minn.:
    Capstone Press, 2006.

Thomas, Pat. *My Manners Matter: A First Look at Being Polite.*
    New York: Barron's, 2006.

On the Web

FactHound offers a safe, fun way to find educator-approved
Internet sites related to this book.

Here's what you do:
1. Visit *www.facthound.com*
2. Choose your grade level.
3. Begin your search.

This book's ID number is 91404853058

Look for all of the books in the Way to Be! Manners series:

Manners at a Friend's House

Manners at School

Manners at the Table

Manners in Public

Manners in the Library

Manners in the Lunchroom

Manners on the Playground

Manners on the School Bus

Manners on the Telephone

Manners with a Library Book

Index